The Intelligible Life:
Why Structure is the Form of Freedom
The Philosophy of Theotic Iteration

by
Sulien Valentino Solovyov

A Note to the Reader: On Rigor and Resistance

The text that follows begins not with an invitation, but with a demand.

This is not a book that aims to comfort or simply affirm the reader's current condition. It is a work of Systematic Hybrid Formalism—a philosophy that requires intellectual effort and structural commitment. It begins, unsparingly, with a foundational axiom that may run counter to contemporary sensibilities, yet is necessary for the system's coherence: the Divine Intelligibility of all reality.

We ask the reader to resist the immediate modern impulse toward Dissolution—the scattering of the self through the rejection of objective structure. Instead, we call for the activation of the Theotic Will, the raw engine within the human soul that yearns not for arbitrary self-creation, but for perfect alignment with enduring truth.

The cost of this system is high: it demands the intellectual fortitude to accept a Moral Axis independent of personal feeling, and the humility to engage in Theotic Iteration—the long, repetitive work of bringing the internal self into fidelity with an external, perfect Norm.

This is not a manual for quick solutions; it is a blueprint for the soul's architecture.

The structure of this entire work rests on a sequence:

This Volume (The Philosophy of Theotic Iteration): Establishes the Law. It defines the Axiom, the Moral Axis, the structure of the Effort and Fallow Cycles, and the necessary rigor of the 80/20 Rule.

The Companion Volume (The Eudaimonic Rhythm): Establishes the Rhythm. It converts the Law into actionable, repeatable disciplines—the tangible practices (from The Linger-Spot to The Hedgerow) that enable a life of integrity.

You must accept the law's demands here before you can successfully wield the rhythm of its practice. Proceed with rigor.

The Editors of The Evergreen Centre

The Intelligible Life: Why Structure is the Form of Freedom-
The Philosophy of Theotic Iteration

by
Sulien Valentino Solovyov

ISBN: 978-1-989647-78-3
First published October 25, 2025
Toronto, Canada

Publisher: The Evergreen Centre
Publisher's Cataloging-in-Publication Data

Solovyov, Sulien Valentino.
    The Intelligible Life : Why Structure is the Form of Freedom / Sulien Valentino Solovyov. — First edition.
    Summary: An anti-nihilistic treatise that introduces Theotic Iteration, a philosophical system synthesizing classical metaphysics with modern existential thought to provide an objective structure for meaning, morality, and purpose.
    Identifiers: ISBN 978-1-989647-78-3
    Subjects: Philosophy—Metaphysics. | Philosophy—Ethics. | Existentialism. | Nihilism—Religious aspects. | Ontology.
    Classification: 111.8—dc23 (Dewey Decimal Classification for Ontology/ Metaphysics of Value)

Chapter I – The Theotic Axiom: Norm, Will, and Telos

The Grounding in Divine Intelligibility

The Philosophy of Theotic Iteration begins with a foundational axiom that serves as its metaphysical and epistemological cornerstone:

Reality is intelligible because it is created by an intelligent God, and human beings are called to participate in that intelligibility.

This axiom is not a blind theological jump but a rational inference concerning the nature of Truth. For **Truth** to be a universal and binding principle—for it to matter absolutely—it cannot be a mere human invention or a statistical average of opinions. Such ultimate authority demands a source beyond human contingency. This necessitates a **personal Absolute**, a transcendent mind whose very essence is **Existence Itself** (Ω, Pure Act), providing a single, perfect source and standard for all truth and meaning.

The Will to Deification

The insistence on this ultimate Norm clarifies the central drive of human existence. The Philosophy of Theotic Iteration affirms the existence of a raw, existential engine—the **Will to Deification** (or **Theotic Will**)—which corresponds to the profound human impulse towards self-overcoming recognized by thinkers like Nietzsche. We do not deny the power of the drive toward mastery; we redirect its object.

Without the foundation of the personal Absolute, the "Will to Power" tragically collapses into arbitrary self-worship and nihilistic chaos. Our system frames human freedom not as the capacity to invent values (Λ), but as the capacity to **align** this intrinsic Theotic Will with the eternal intelligibility that gives it meaning and trajectory. The human person is summoned not to rebel, but to engage in the **continual work of iteration**—aligning thought, action, and being to the divine source. This choice for alignment is the very meaning of knowledge, morality, and authentic life.

The Aesthetics of Intelligibility

The grounding in Divine Intelligibility extends immediately to the physical and perceptual world, transforming our understanding of beauty and creation. If reality possesses a divine structure, that structure must be perceptible, making **Aesthetics** a core branch of epistemology.

True Beauty is defined as the maximal localized expression of Divine Intelligibility. It is not a subjective pleasure, but an **objective, perceptual measure** of being aligning with the (Divine Reason). This leads to a **Metaphysics of Aesthetic Scarcity**: The human vocation, particularly through art, craft, and technology, is to overcome the chaotic entropy of an under-formed creation.

The artist is a **co-creator** whose work is an active, structured iteration—a hard-won victory that momentarily forces matter into a more perfect and intense mirroring of the divine. Beauty, therefore, is a profound testament to the effort of (Δ).

The Cosmic Telos of Theotic Iteration

The ultimate implication of the Theotic Axiom—that reality is intelligently created and co-created by humanity—culminates in the final, embodied destiny of all things. The goal is not an escape from creation, but the **Transfiguration of Creation itself**.

This vision stands against philosophies that dismiss the material world as secondary or corruptible. does not lead to a disembodied state; rather, it implies the **Glorification of Form**. The final "iteration" of existence will be the **Universal Resurrection**, where the human person is restored as a perfected, immortal unity of soul and **Purified Body**.

Crucially, this individual perfection is mirrored by the cosmos. The entire natural order—the "earth" that humanity was called to join in making—will be transformed into the New Heavens and New Earth (χ). This Cosmic Telos (ultimate goal) confirms the transcendent value of the human creative vocation: every sincere act of art, craft, morality, and inquiry performed through Theotic Iteration is a genuine participation in the eternal making of a fully realized, physically manifest Divine Kingdom. The purpose of existence is thus a perfected embodiment in a perfected reality.

Aphorism:
"Without the Creator, man must pretend to be one. But the part wears thin, and the mask slips. The Theotic Will is not to be a god, but to be perfected in God."

Chapter II: Objective Reality and Created Reality

In the unfolding tapestry of existence, two fundamental realms intertwine and define human experience: **Objective Reality** and **Created Reality**. These are not mere abstractions but living, dynamic orders that shape everything from the simplest act of knowing to the grandest pursuit of meaning. The Philosophy of Theotic Iteration holds these realms as coexisting dimensions, essential and irreducible.

The Necessity of Two Orders: A Philosophical and Theological Imperative

To posit one reality alone is to fall victim to reductionism and either despair or illusion. Materialism collapses all into the temporal, dismissing the eternal as fantasy; radical idealism or solipsism elevates subjective perception to the status of all reality, condemning truth to mere opinion.

Orthodox Christian theology, as articulated by St. Gregory Palamas, illuminates this duality from the heights of mystical experience. St. Gregory distinguishes between God's essence— completely transcendent and unreachable—and His energies— accessible and immanent, revealing Himself to creation without compromising His transcendence. This difference grounds the theological affirmation that God is both wholly other and intimately present. Similarly, Theotic Iteration asserts that **Objective Reality** is like God's essence—unchanging, perfect, eternal—while **Created Reality** corresponds loosely to the energies, the unfolding manifestations in time and space where human freedom and creativity dwell.

St. Maximus the Confessor deepens this vision in his writings on cosmic synergy: the entire cosmos is alive in a purposeful divine dialogue where created beings participate willingly in divine energy, transforming through grace. For Maximus, Created

Reality is not a shadow to be discarded but the field of divine-human cooperation.
It is here that we encounter the human: the liminal, tension-filled place where becoming meets being, where the eternal presses into the temporal.

Dialogue: St. Benedict and Ralph Waldo Emerson on the Duality of Being

Imagine a quiet conversation in the cloister of a Benedictine monastery between the saints and sages of different times. St. Benedict, wise practitioner of ordered life, turns to Ralph Waldo Emerson, the seer of the American transcendental spirit.

St. Benedict:
"Brother Emerson, your writings speak of the 'Over-Soul' from which all flows, yet you exalt the self's unfolding above all. Here, we believe the path lies in obedience—not merely to law but to the Divine order manifest in God Himself. Stability and humility protect the soul's journey toward becoming one with that Over-Being, which is beyond us, yet within."

Emerson:
"Indeed, Father Benedict, the Self is fluent, expansive—a river trying to meet the sea of the Universal Spirit. But your monastic rule grounds that flow in discipline, loyalty to the eternal pattern beneath the flux. This echoes the necessity of order amid change. The 'Over-Soul' is like your Objective Reality, vast and enduring, while the individual's daily struggle embodies what your Rule calls 'conversatio morum'—the ongoing conversion and transformation within the created world."

St. Benedict:
"The monastery is the microcosm where this dialogue happens—the music of prayer and labor, the balance of solitude and community—a rehearsal of the soul's ascent from Created Reality back into communion with God."

This imagined encounter reveals two complementary perspectives: the transcendental intuition of Emerson and the practical, lived wisdom of Benedict, both affirming the harmony between eternal truth and temporal becoming.

Analogies to Illuminate the Duality

Throughout human history, the dualism of order and participation has been encoded in metaphor:

- **Music:** Objective Reality is akin to the musical score—immutable, perfect, prescribing the structure and harmony. Created Reality is the performance—the temporal unfolding in real time, subject to variations, mistakes, interpretations, and becoming. The musician's role is to bridge score and sound, bringing divine order to life, yet always with freedom to play.
- **Architecture:** The heavenly blueprint is eternal and perfect; the constructed building is temporal, shaped by hands that can err or innovate. The craftsman's vocation is to manifest the perfect idea into the contingent world without losing its integrity.
- **Science:** Laws of nature exist as stable truths; phenomena are the transient, contingent events governed by those laws. Scientists discover laws (Objective Reality) and test hypotheses in experiments (Created Reality), iterating closer to understanding through continual feedback.

Such analogies help clarify that to live fully is to inhabit the tension of these two orders, not to collapse them.

The Human Role: More Than Passive Witness

Humans do not stand neutral before these realities; rather, they are **agents of mediation and transformation.** The human person, made in the image of God, possesses a unique freedom to align Created Reality with Objective Reality.

The Cappadocian Fathers taught that humanity's likeness to God involves participation (μετοχή) in divine energies—an active sharing and extension of God's creative life. This participation is not passive acceptance but a vocation to co-create, to build beauty, bring justice, and grow in truth.

Simultaneously, Eastern Orthodoxy's emphasis on theosis (deification) highlights human becoming as the journey toward perfect communion with God, the Source of Objective Reality, through free and loving cooperation.

The Dangers of Collapsing the Two Realities

When civilizations collapse the distinction, the results are catastrophic:

- **Materialism and Neo-Gnosticism** reduce reality to mere matter or a false spiritual abstraction, leading either to nihilism or escapism.
- **Extreme Skepticism or Subjectivism** denies any stable truth, fostering relativism and social fragmentation.
- **Totalitarian ideologies** claim absolute truth but impose rigid worldly systems that negate freedom and suppress the creative iteration essential to human dignity.

G. K. Chesterton, the master of paradox and Christian wit, warns against the tendency to "flatten" reality for convenience:
"The whole modern world has divided itself into Conservatives and Progressives. The business of Progressives is to go on making mistakes. The business of Conservatives is to prevent the mistakes from being corrected." In other words, denying the eternal truth or the historical process impoverishes both.

Chesterton's ironic insight points to the necessity of holding to both eternal norms and creative movement.

Concluding Reflection and Dialogue with G. K. Chesterton

In a garden, a monk meets Chesterton:

Monk:
"Sir, your paradoxes point to a deeper truth: that faith and reason, tradition and innovation, silence and speech, are not antagonists but dance partners in the divine theatre."

Chesterton:
"Precisely. To be human is to navigate this beautiful tension—to be both rooted and wandering. The dual orders aren't enemies; they are the twin wings on which the soul flies."

Aphorism:
"What is, forever is. What becomes, forever invites."

Chapter III – The Living Process of Knowing: Multi-Nodal Iteration

The philosophy of Theotic Iteration fundamentally redefines knowledge as **a living, active process**. Knowledge is neither static accumulation nor passive reception but **a dynamic, multi-nodal iterative engagement with reality**. Where traditional epistemology has often either veered toward skeptical uncertainty or rigid dogmatism, here knowing is cast as a continuous dance: a series of well-placed steps toward ever-deeper truth.

This dialectic unfolds between two poles: **Discovery** (the uncovering of eternal, unchanging truths which lie in **Objective Reality**) and **Co-creation** (the creative bringing forth of new forms within Created Reality, which resonate and harmonize with those eternal principles). Our epistemic journey thus unfolds in a feedback loop of posing, testing, refining, and re-aligning—a process that is inherently communal, multifaceted, and iterative.

Defining Multi-Nodal Iteration

By "multi-nodal," Theotic Iteration means that the search for knowledge is pursued simultaneously from multiple vantage points, or **Nodes of Knowing**. These nodes are the specific human faculties through which the Theotic Will engages reality.
No single node suffices alone; the full picture emerges only by integrating their feedback, much as a symphony requires many instruments playing in coordinated harmony. This approach respects both the a priori (what reason reveals prior to experience) and the a posteriori (what experience discloses) without confusing or collapsing the two.

The necessary **Nodes of Knowing** are:
- **Reason:** Logical analysis, metaphysics, and coherent thought uncover objective principles.

- **Sense Experience:** Empiricism reveals how principles manifest contingently in the physical world.
- **Memory and Tradition:** The communal storehouse of tested wisdom, guiding and correcting new claims.
- **Intuition:** The inner compass aligning understanding beyond discursive reason.
- **Aesthetic Insight:** Beauty discloses objective splendor and coherence unknown to cold intellect, engaging the Glorification of Form.
- **Revelation:** The special mode by which God discloses Himself, acting as the ultimate boundary condition and compass for all other nodes.

These nodes challenge and correct the others, forming a robust, self-correcting pathway to ever-expanding knowledge.

Iteration in Practice: Science, Art, and Spirit

These iterative nodes mirror the cycles of scientific experimentation, artistic refinement, and spiritual discipline:

- **Iteration in Science: The Mirror of Reality** Scientific inquiry epitomizes the process of iteration. Hypotheses emerge, tested against the "testing ground" of Objective Reality, and reshaped by experiments, failures, and refinements. This process embodies multi-nodal iteration, as data, peer review, and theoretical consistency each serve as nodes feeding back into conceptual schemes. Scientific iteration models a metaphysical harmony between human reason and the intelligible order created by God.

- **Iteration in Art: The Garment of the Eternal Artists** live iteration, sketching, painting, and carving—their creation evolving in dialogue with their vision, the medium, and the Aesthetics of Intelligibility. Creating a work of art is a feedback loop between the eternal ideals of beauty and the mutable canvas of time-bound form. Art's iterative nature reveals that knowing includes feeling and imagination alongside pure intellect, as the artist co-creates form that mirrors the divine.

Iteration in Spiritual Discipline: Progress Toward Theosis In spiritual life, iteration appears in the repetitive disciplines of prayer, fasting, and repentance. The soul moves step by recursive step toward holiness, shedding falsehood and echoing God's grace. Monastic rules and sacramental life are forms of multi-nodal iteration where scripture, tradition, community, and interior experience test and deepen the soul's knowledge of God and progress toward Theosis.

Iteration vs. Skepticism and Dogmatism

Theotic Iteration refuses the paralysis of endless skepticism, which suspends judgment indefinitely and thereby forfeits knowledge. Yet it also rejects the presumptuous closure of dogmatism that would claim finality without testing and renewal. Iteration inhabits a middle path—a disciplined openness to correction and growth balanced with firm commitment to the real.

Dialogue: St. Maximus the Confessor and Ralph Waldo Emerson on Knowing

Maximus: "True knowledge comes from participation in the Divine energies—the living flow by which God reveals Himself. The mind is a vessel both filled and pouring forth, ever discovering eternal truth and co-creating within the temporal." Emerson: "Yes, the soul's progression is a continual creation, forever reaching beyond itself. But the Over-Soul, the infinite spring, requires that our fluent Will submit to the discipline of the eternal pattern. Reason must listen; the heart must commune." Maximus and Emerson together depict knowledge not as inert possession but as a vital interplay between being known and knowledge given.

Aphorism:

"The lie can be invented once; the truth requires rehearsal."

Chapter IV – The Moral Axis: Creation vs. Dissolution
The Ontology of Moral Reality

To speak of ethics is ultimately to speak of **being itself**. The Philosophy of Theotic Iteration understands morality as an orientation within the very fabric of existence: a moral axis between **creation and dissolution**.

Being is good because it participates in God, the source of all existence and perfection. Every increase or affirmation of being aligns with the divine will to create and sustain. Conversely, **dissolution** is a movement away from fullness—to fragmentation, decay, and non-being—an **ontological privation**.

This metaphysical framing goes beyond legalism or mere virtue ethics; it grounds right and wrong in the real participation or rejection of divine life.

The Creation Pole: Acts of Building and Affirmation

Creation is anything that fosters life, order, beauty, justice, compassion, knowledge, and hope. It is the unfolding of potentialities in harmony with eternal truth.
In tangible culture, take the soaring spires of **Chartres Cathedral**.

The faithful built this over generations, weaving stone, glass, and prayer into a cosmos of light and sound. This is moral creation writ large: composing harmony from chaos, touching the eternal through temporal craft. Likewise, the abolition of slavery was a creative breakthrough—an extension of justice into social structures previously mired in dissolution. Even small acts—the patient nurture of a child, the minute composition of a sonnet— participate in this axis, reflecting the boundless creative will of God.

The Dissolution Pole: Fragmentation and Decay

Dissolution is the ontological failure: the breaking down of unity, the stifling of life, the corrosion of trust and beauty.

Culturally, one sees it in the degradation of the Roman Empire's civic virtue, in the propaganda that twists truth for power, or in policies that rip apart the social fabric. Spiritually, **evil is privation** — a withholding of grace, a dark withdrawal from love. Mortal sin fractures the soul's harmony, leading downward on the axis.

Dialogue: G.K. Chesterton and St. Maximus the Confessor on Moral Goodness Chesterton: "Goodness is a lively, constructive force — the joy of building a world worthy of children to inherit. Evil is the dull, envious scratch of a corrupt soul breaking what others have wrought." Maximus: "To walk the path of righteousness is to join in God's cosmic work, weaving creation's scattered fragments back into the unity of divine love." This dialogue encapsulates how moral action, in this philosophy, is a cosmic artistry — every act painting or erasing the tapestry of being.

Moral Habits and the Ascent of Theosis

Theotic Iteration insists that morality is a practice — habits of mind and heart that cultivate creation or facilitate dissolution. Patience, generosity, humility, and courage are habits that nurture creative being. Conversely, pride, cruelty, sloth, and despair feed dissolution.

Sanctification, or theosis, is not a passive gift but an active, lifelong commitment to inhabit the creative pole — learning again and again to choose life.

St. Benedict's Wisdom on Moral Habit Formation In his famous Rule, St. Benedict instructs the novice to "take care that nothing goes before the Work of God." This underscores the primacy of aligning daily action with the divine will — a repeated choosing of creation and consecration over fragmentation. The monastic life becomes a laboratory of the moral axis, where one steadily learns to unmake the habits of dissolution and remake the habits of creation.

The Moral Axis in Society and Culture

Communities and nations reflect this axis in their laws, customs, and cultural products. A just society is one that fosters the moral habit of creation within its citizens, providing education, freedom, justice, and beauty scaffolding for flourishing. Corrupt societies institutionalize dissolution—enacting systemic injustice, crushing creativity, or fostering cynicism and alienation.

Parable: The Sculptor and the Vandal Imagine two figures before a block of marble. The **sculptor** sees the form within, patiently chipping away, revealing hidden beauty. The **vandal** strikes randomly, smashing what might have been. Human freedom stands before the raw material of life—the choice to sculpt or destroy echoes daily in thought, word, and deed.

The Ultimate Ethical Goal: Union with Divine Creation

The moral axis culminates in **theosis**—becoming more fully like God by embracing creation in all its fullness. Every creative act, from the smallest kindness to the grandest architecture, is a step toward this union. Through grace, what begins in human effort ripens into divine participation.

Aphorism:
"What the hand builds, the heart becomes."

Chapter V – Beauty as Ontological Signature: The Perceptual Form of Theosis

Introduction: Beauty Transcending Subjectivity

In an age saturated with relativism, where beauty is often reduced to mere opinion or fleeting fashion, the Philosophy of Theotic Iteration boldly reclaims beauty as **objective and ontological** — an intrinsic quality that manifests the divine order embedded in reality itself. Beauty is not an optional byproduct or subjective luxury; it is the **perceptual self-revelation** of **Objective Reality**, offering a glimpse through which the eternal Logos shines into the temporal.

As the ancient Greeks sought the *kalon* — the beautiful that is also good and true — so this philosophy holds beauty inseparable from goodness and truth, each reflecting and enfolding the others. Beauty is the aesthetic evidence that the universe is not chaotic, but designed for our ascent.

The Three Pillars of Beauty and the Process of Theosis

Beauty, as a real and measurable quality, unfolds in three fundamental dimensions that correspond directly to the coherence and purpose of creation:

- **Integrity: Wholeness and coherence within a thing or act.** It means every part exists in organic unity, nothing fragmented or false. Integrity reflects the **perfection of divine essence** and serves as the foundation upon which beauty rests. In the human spirit, Integrity is the necessary starting point of **Purification** (κα'θαρσις).
- **Proportion: The fitting relation between parts and to the whole.** Proper measure and harmony reveal order — not mechanical symmetry but a living, dynamic consonance

21

akin to the golden ratio or sacred geometry, resonating with the deeper structure of creation. Proportion is the physical manifestation of **Intelligibility** and guides the human process of **Iteration** and alignment.

- **Radiance: The emanation of light, truth, and life beyond mere form.** Radiance is what causes beauty to move the soul, to beckon, to invite participation beyond the immediate object itself. Radiance is the perceptual manifestation of **uncreated energies** and serves as the **visible sign of Theosis** (Deification/Glorification).

These three together define the **ontological signature of beauty** as a participation in the divine life.

Dialogue: St. Gregory Palamas and Ralph Waldo Emerson on True Beauty

St. Gregory Palamas:
"Beauty is not merely form, but the uncreated light illuminating the depths. To behold true beauty is to experience the divine energies, a foretaste of the heavenly kingdom."

Emerson:
"Yes, beauty is the expression of the Infinite in finite forms. When I stand in the presence of nature's majesty, I glimpse the Over-Soul's eternal breath made manifest in stone and leaf."

This dialogue unites the Orthodox vision of beauty as revelation of uncreated light with Emerson's transcendental intuition of infinite and finite merging in nature's beauty.

The Role of Beauty in Christian Art and Iconography

The Orthodox tradition illustrates its conviction in objective beauty through the theology and practice of iconography. Icons are not mere paintings but windows into the divine, crafted with exacting proportions and symbolic forms to communicate truth beyond words.

They embody integrity in their consistency through centuries, proportion in sacred geometry and placement, and radiance in their gold leaf and color symbolism—all inviting contemplation and ascent toward the eternal.

This sacred art resists relativism and kitsch by its rootedness in revealed truth.

False Beauty and The Idolatry of Appearance

Not all that glitters is truly beautiful. False beauty—in the form of kitsch, propaganda, or hollow glamor—seduces by superficiality and artifice, leading the soul astray.

Chesterton famously highlighted this danger:
"The whole modern world has explained Christianity away by explaining it away." In other words, false beauty often masquerades as truth but carves idols from the ephemeral, distracting from genuine transcendence.

Kitsch vulgarizes the sacred; propaganda weaponizes aesthetics; glamor masks decay.

Recognizing and resisting false beauty is itself a moral and spiritual act of creation.

Beauty as Evangelism and Invitation

Beauty does not coerce but draws. Its power is a gentle persuasion to aligned life.

Encountering true beauty awakens the soul, moves the heart, and awakens a longing for the divine source.

Where laws and words may provoke resistance, beauty invites without violence.

Consider the transforming effect of great art in troubled societies—how radiant spaces and exquisite music have welcomed hope and restored dignity.

Emerson and Chesterton on Beauty and the Human Spirit
Emerson:

"Beauty is the ultimate rebuke to despair, the quiet assurance that the universe is shaped by meaning, not chaos."

Chesterton:
"To see the world in a grain of sand is to laugh at cynicism. Beauty renews wonder, and wonder renews faith."

Their voices remind us that beauty is not mere surface but the spiritual oxygen of imagination and hope.

Practical Implications: Living Beauty as Moral Action

Theotic Iteration insists that beauty must be embodied.
Our homes, communities, work, and liturgies should reflect integrity, proportion, and radiance.

Small acts—tending a garden, telling a truthful story, maintaining dignity in speech—are iterations of beauty that build toward divine communion.

Thus beauty becomes a moral habit and a sacred vocation, infusing aesthetics with ethics and vice versa.

St. Benedict's Contemplation on Beauty's Order

St. Benedict:
"Let prayer and work be done in due time, with order and harmony, that all things may give glory to God. For to dwell in beauty is to dwell in His peace."

His rule guides the daily ordering of life as an echo of heaven's order; the very rhythm of the monastic day is an iterative harmony of beauty lived.

Aphorism:
"A false beauty is an idol; a true beauty is a window."

Chapter VI – Anthropology: The Apprentice of God
Humanity's Vocation in Theotic Iteration

The Human Being Beyond Reduction

The modern world is adept at reducing humanity to something smaller than it truly is. To the materialist, man is a biochemical accident; to the cynic, a social animal chasing status; to the machine-minded technocrat, a problem to be optimized. The Philosophy of Theotic Iteration rejects all such diminutions.

In its vision, the human being is neither an accident nor a mere tool of nature, but a living icon of God, fashioned in His image (imago Dei) for the purpose of growth toward His likeness (similitude). This growth is never merely moral self-improvement; it is vocational — the craft of aligning our will, our imagination, our making, and our loving with the Creator's own work.

Man is not here to substitute for God or to rival Him; man is here to apprentice under Him.

Apprenticeship as Theological Anthropology

The idea of apprenticeship differs radically from mere productivity or obedience.

An apprentice watches, learns, imitates, and gradually begins to work with the master's skill — not to replace the master, but to become more fully capable of expressing his mastery. In the context of divine apprenticeship:

- God's Objective Reality is the eternal model.
- Created Reality is the workshop.
- The human life is the practicum — the years spent learning to build in a way that reflects the eternal blueprint.

The Orthodox Fathers often spoke of the human journey in these terms. St. Irenaeus' remark that "the glory of God is man fully alive" expresses the idea that human flourishing is not an accident but the deliberate result of God's ongoing formation of His apprentice.

Freedom as Tool and Test

Freedom is essential to this apprenticeship. A coerced apprentice can mimic steps, but will not grasp the principles. God insists on our freedom — not as bare choice detached from truth, but as the ability to enact our proper telos.

In this vision, freedom has two aspects:

1. Freedom From — the liberty from coercion, oppression, and the binding power of sin.

2. Freedom For — the liberty to create, love, and act in harmony with the eternal order.

Without the second, the first is hollow. The world often idolizes "freedom from" while neglecting "freedom for," leaving people adrift without telos, a boat cut loose from both dock and rudder.

Dialogue: St. Benedict and G.K. Chesterton on Work and Joy

St. Benedict: "The man who labors faithfully in humility learns more than the work of his hands. He learns the cadence of God's order. *Ora et labora* — pray and work — is no drudgery but a song whose verses echo in eternity."

Chesterton:
"And the joy! For the created world is not a prison but a playground — albeit one in which the game has rules. To create within the Creator's order is to play the divine game, and the score is kept in love."

This imagined exchange fuses Benedict's disciplined vision with Chesterton's joyous paradox: the workshop of God is also His playground, and to apprentice under Him is to marry discipline with delight.

The Moral Responsibility of Creativity

Within Theotic Iteration, creativity is not optional self-expression — it is a moral responsibility. To be given image-bearing status is to carry the duty to shape the world in ways that increase integrity, proportion, and radiance.

Where creation is neglected, dissolution seeps in. A garden untended becomes chokehold for weeds; a culture untended becomes a circus of triviality and decay.

Responsibility here means that one's work — whether as poet, parent, farmer, legislator, or scientist — must be measured against the eternal blueprint.

Emerson's Voice: The Individual as World-Maker

Emerson, though outside the Christian tradition, perceived that every person is a world-maker of sorts. In *Self-Reliance* he writes: *"Every man is tasked to make his life, even in its details, worthy of the contemplation of his most elevated and critical hour."*

Theotic Iteration agrees, while grounding Emerson's intuition: our "most elevated hour" is not self-generated, but our closest moment of alignment with the divine order.

The Parable of the Two Apprentices

In a small carpentry shop, two apprentices are given rough timber and the master's design.

- The first studies the design, asks the master questions, and shapes the wood with care. His bench is covered in shavings, but the piece emerging in his hands matches the blueprint — alive with skill and beauty.
- The second ignores the design, opting to "express himself" without regard for function or proportion. At the day's end, his work collapses under its own strain.

The Created Reality offers both apprentices the same raw materials and the same time. Their outcomes depend entirely on their relationship to the Objective pattern and their willingness to be taught.

Human Life as Collaborative Art

From this perspective, every human life is a unique commission — a collaborative artwork between the soul and God. No two commissions are identical, but all must be true to the Architect's vision.

That is why Theotic Iteration rejects comparisons that belittle the individuality of vocation. A monk's iteration may be expressed in liturgical prayer, a baker's in bread that nourishes body and spirit, a musician's in works that marry beauty with meaning. All are equally necessary, all equally under apprenticeship.

How Failure Functions in Apprenticeship

In a true apprenticeship, mistakes are not merely tolerated — they are essential. They reveal gaps in understanding, invite the master's correction, and eventually lead to mastery.

Within Theotic Iteration, sin and error, while destructive, can be repurposed through repentance into profound stages of learning. A planed board cut too short teaches more than one cut carelessly correct.

The key is humility: the willingness to accept correction and iterate again.

Conclusion: The Dignity of the Apprentice

Every human bears this high calling: to be an apprentice under the Master of the cosmos. This dignity resists all attempts to reduce man to consumer, cog, or accident.

The apprentice's task is lifelong: receiving, practicing, failing, refining, and finally creating in unbroken harmony with the master's will. This is the human story — an apprenticeship destined to culminate in theosis, where the apprentice and the master share the same light.

Aphorism:
"We were not made to rival God, but to rhyme with Him."

Chapter VII – The Just Society as the Forge of Creation
The Social Dimension of Theotic Iteration

While the human person is the central actor in Theotic Iteration, life is always lived in community. The well-being of individuals depends deeply on the social and political structures within which they exist. Therefore, a philosophy of human flourishing must account for the just society—not abstractly, but as an essential enabler and protector of creative iteration.

The society is not simply a backdrop or container for human action; it is the forge where individual and collective vocations are shaped, refined, and expressed. A just society must maximize the conditions for iterative creation, ensuring individuals can pursue the divine likeness through free, disciplined, and meaningful acts.

Freedom and Order: The Delicate Balance

Theotic Iteration insists that freedom alone is insufficient; without order, freedom devolves into chaos or nihilism. Similarly, order without freedom becomes tyranny and stifles creativity.

Freedom here connotes more than absence from constraint; it is the presence of authentic capacity to act toward true goods. Meanwhile, order is not mere control but a framework — laws, customs, traditions — that protect and nurture creative flourishing.

The political philosopher John Locke argued that civil government's role was to protect natural rights, but Theotic Iteration extends this: the state's highest purpose is to safeguard the workshop of the soul, enabling iterative co-creation with God.

Dialogue: St. Benedict and Ralph Waldo Emerson on Society and the Individual

St. Benedict:
"In the monastery, structure and rule do not limit the soul; they free it to seek God without distraction. The balance of work, prayer, and rest models a society that honors the Creator's order."

Emerson:
"True society must respect the individual's creative impulse; if it binds too tightly, it asphyxiates the soul. Yet without some harmony and rule, it dissolves into the wilderness of anarchy."

Their perspectives together illuminate the tension between liberty and order, urging societies to find rhythm, not rigidity.

Institutions as Enablers or Suppressors of Iteration

Institutions—educational, legal, religious, economic—are the scaffolding through which cultural and individual creativity is either nurtured or crushed.

- Enabling institutions provide justice, education, and opportunity, protect conscience, foster virtue, and encourage innovation consistent with moral truth.

- Suppressive institutions impose dogmatic uniformity, deny freedom of thought or action, or commodify and degrade creativity into mere productivity.

Totalitarian regimes exemplify suppression, where a false singular truth is violently imposed, extinguishing the iterative spirit.

The Moral Bankruptcy of Collectivist Tyranny

Collectivism's fatal flaw in Theotic Iteration's framework is that it denies the individual's divine vocation to co-create. By subordinating all to the state's will—or to ideologies posing as ultimate realities—it enforces dissolution at social scale.

The monks of Eastern Orthodoxy, especially under Byzantine rule, knew this well; their resistance to state intrusion into spiritual life exemplifies the sacred boundary between political authority and personal conscience. Without such boundaries, society loses its creative soul.

The Role of Justice and Charity in Society

Justice in this philosophy is not blind equality nor mere retributive fairness, but the active ordering of society toward the common good and flourishing of all. Charity complements justice by motivating generosity beyond mere obligation.

True justice ensures that each person can play their unique orchestral part in the symphony of society, contributing their created gifts toward a harmonious whole.

Chesterton's Paradox of Progress and Conservatism

G.K. Chesterton:
"Progress without order invites chaos; conservatism without progress invites death. The living society balances preservation with renewal."

This paradox warns societies against extremes—the impulsiveness of reckless change or the stubbornness of fossilized tradition. The just social order is iterative, perpetually reforming, never stationary.

The Cultural Mandate and Political Responsibility

The biblical cultural mandate *(Genesis 1:28)* teaches that humanity is called to till and keep the earth, shaping creation in partnership with God.

Extrapolated, this implies political authority is stewardship, not dominion. Leaders are the apprentices of a higher order with responsibility to guard, nurture, and order the public workshop.

Good governance enhances freedom, protects truth, and fosters beauty—the three pillars of Theotic Iteration.

Practical Political Implications

- Protect freedom of conscience, speech, and innovation.
- Foster environments for education that integrate faith, reason, and creativity.

- Create laws that mirror divine justice — favoring restoration over retribution.
- Encourage arts, sciences, and professions as vocations rather than mere jobs.

Ignoring these imperatives invites dissolution on civic scales — corruption, despair, nihilism.

Vision: Society as a Community of Saints and Sinners in Iteration

The just society is a mosaic of imperfect persons united in a shared effort — a community of saints and sinners engaged in collective iteration toward divine order.

It does not expect perfection but repentance and growth, cooperation and contest, dialogue and discipline.

This is society as a workshop for human sanctification, echoing St. Benedict's monastic ideal writ large.

Aphorism:
"The first duty of the state is to protect the workshop of the soul."

Chapter VIII – Theodicy: Suffering as Signal

The Problem of Suffering in Theotic Iteration

Suffering has tormented humanity's reflection on God since the dawn of reason. How can a good and omnipotent Creator permit pain, evil, and death? The Philosophy of Theotic Iteration confronts this age-old question not by abstract speculation alone, but by framing suffering within the dynamic, iterative cosmos where free will, creation, and correction interact.

Rather than denying or minimizing suffering, Theotic Iteration sees suffering as an intrinsic feedback mechanism within Created Reality: a signal that reveals misalignment either in individual choice or in communal structures.

Suffering as Feedback, Not Final Cause

Suffering is not the cause of evil nor an expression of Divine cruelty, but a consequence of departing from the eternal order. It is the natural recoil against sin and disorder, morally and ontologically corrective.

Like a fever in the body, suffering calls attention to imbalance that demands healing. This shifts suffering from being an inscrutable punishment to a message: reality itself "speaks back" to those who stray.

Dialogue: St. John Chrysostom and G.K. Chesterton on Suffering
St. John Chrysostom:

"Even in affliction, the faithful find a school for virtue and hope. The Cross is the greatest lesson — a paradox where death births eternal life."

Chesterton:
"Suffering baffles the intellect but ennobles the soul. It sharpens the edges that dull complacency and invites the heart into deeper wonder."

Through their dialogue, suffering reveals itself as the crucible of transformation, sanctifying even the darkest experiences within Divine love.

The Voluntary and Involuntary Dimensions of Suffering

Some suffering is self-inflicted—the product of misguided choices, moral failings, or neglect. This suffering signals the need for repentance and growth.

Other suffering is imposed from outside—injustices, violence, natural disasters—which tests endurance, invokes solidarity, and calls forth creative response. Martyrdom exemplifies the apex of this response: the refusal to let dissolution triumph.

The Diabolical Inversion: Those Who Feed on Suffering

The Philosophy of Theotic Iteration identifies one of the gravest moral failures as the delight in others' suffering—sadism, cruelty, and tyranny that torment not for gain but for destruction.

These "vampires of suffering" embody ultimate dissolution, opposing the Divine Will to create and sustain.

Yet even here, the feedback function of suffering remains: victims are given a sign—to resist, escape, or transform the evil.

The Role of Grace and Redemption

Suffering, while real and often terrible, is not the final word. Through grace, the iterative process can transmute pain into growth, death into life, and brokenness into beauty.

The Cross is the very model of this transformation—the greatest iteration in history where suffering is overcome not by denial but by sacrificial love, ushering in resurrection.

Reflection: Monastic Endurance and Theosis

Within the monastic tradition, suffering is embraced as a path of purification and union. The Rule of St. Benedict instructs endurance tempered by hope, with prayer and community as anchors.

The spiritual disciplines are iterative responses to suffering— repeatedly orienting the self toward God despite pain, thus turning suffering into steppingstones of sanctification.

Emerson's View: Suffering as a Teacher

Emerson noted that hardship refines the soul:
"Adversity is the first path to truth."

While secular in tone, his insight harmonizes with Theotic Iteration's view that suffering challenges complacency, ignites creativity in response, and deepens appreciation for beauty and goodness.

Practical and Communal Implications

Recognizing suffering as a signal reshapes responses:

- Encouraging compassionate action and systemic reform.
- Rejecting simplistic moralizing or fatalism.
- Embracing endurance and hope balanced with active resistance to dissolution.

Communities become workshops of healing and creative resilience, embodying the iterative call.

Aphorism:
"Pain that points is a teacher; pain that feeds is a parasite."

Chapter IX – Dialogue With The Greats: Engaging Nietzsche, Kierkegaard, Sartre, and Others in Theotic Iteration's Light

Introduction: The Necessity of Dialogue

Every profound philosophical system must answer the great thinkers who have shaped the questions of meaning, existence, and freedom. The Philosophy of Theotic Iteration does not reject the challenges posed by Nietzsche, Kierkegaard, or Sartre; instead, it embraces and transcends them by situating human freedom and creativity within a theistic frame of iterative participation.

This chapter stages a series of reflective dialogues, juxtaposing Theotic Iteration's affirmations with the critiques and insights of these intellectual titans.

Nietzsche: From the Death of God to the Eternal Creation

Nietzsche proclaimed the death of God and the consequent "will to power" as the creative force of man making his own values. Yet this birth of the Übermensch rings hollow in Theotic Iteration due to the absence of grounding in eternal truth.

Theotic Iteration responds:

1. Values are not arbitrarily made but discovered and extended in alignment with Objective Reality.

2. Human greatness is found not in solitary rebellion but in participation with the Divine Artist—co-creation informed by eternal order.

3. The will to power is rightly the will to align freedom toward true good, not mere force.

Dialogue:
Nietzsche:
"Man must become god to escape his nihilism."

Theotic Iteration:
"Man need not usurp God but must apprentice to Him—allowing his power to be perfected in divine partnership."

Through this dialogue emerges a re-envisioning of power as cooperative rather than adversarial.

Kierkegaard: Faith Beyond Reason or Reason Fulfilled?

Kierkegaard saw the leap of faith as a personal, existential necessity beyond reason and ethics—sometimes absurd. Theotic Iteration, while affirming the existential seriousness Kierkegaard diagnosed, reframes faith as the culmination of reason's ascent to the personal Absolute.

Faith is no irrational gamble but the natural next step when reason encounters the personal, loving God who invites co-creation.

Dialogue:
Kierkegaard:
"Faith is the absurd leap beyond ethical universality."

Theotic Iteration:
"Faith is the synthesis of all prior knowledge, where reason and love dance in personal commitment."

Thus, faith is the final iterative act of understanding, not its overthrow.

Sartre: Essence and Existence Revisited

Sartre's dictum "existence precedes essence" posits radical freedom but leaves humans condemned to create meaning alone. Theotic Iteration disagrees fundamentally: essence is given—in the divine image—and freedom is the capacity to embrace or reject that gift.

This restores meaning as pre-inscribed, while affirming the preciousness of human agency within that framework.

Dialogue:

Sartre:
"Man is condemned to be free; there is no given essence."

Theotic Iteration:
"Man is graced with essence, but through freedom must co-create its full expression."

Freedom is challenging precisely because it is a freedom for sanctified participation, not arbitrary construction.

Dostoevsky: Suffering as Correction to Arbitrary Will

Dostoevsky's tortured and brilliant characters—the radical experimenters like Raskolnikov or Ivan Karamazov—exist precisely where Theotic Iteration warns against: the tragic collapse into Dissolution. His protagonists attempt to perform acts of arbitrary self-will, trying to invent a new moral reality where a governing structure has been rejected. This drive is the corrupted expression of the Will to Deification; without the foundation of the Moral Axis (Λ), the impulse toward self-mastery descends into nihilistic self-worship.

In Dostoevsky's universe, suffering functions as the necessary corrective. The psychological agony experienced by the transgressor is the world's forced reminder that human freedom is not the capacity to invent values, but the painful, humbling capacity to align with the enduring intelligibility that already exists. Redemption, therefore, is not a grand, singular conversion, but a slow, excruciating Iteration (Δ) back toward the objective Λ that was violently defied.

Lewis: Joyful Assent and Structural Integrity

C.S. Lewis complements this vision of corrective suffering by providing the intellectual necessity of the system. Through his reasoned apologetics and fantasy, Lewis establishes the inevitability of the Absolute Source (Ω)—the personal Absolute whose very essence guarantees that reality is intelligible. He provides the logical groundwork for the Moral Axis (Λ), asserting that structural truth must exist for any form of moral or rational life to hold meaning.

Furthermore, Lewis's spiritual writings affirm the system's approach to effort and rest. He advocates for disciplined commitment and the joyful assent required to follow a divine order. His work validates the need for a Fallow Cycle—a time of surrender, withdrawal, and waiting—proving that spiritual and intellectual health is sustained through rhythm and structure, not by chaotic, uninterrupted striving.

The Redemptive Power of Iterative Change

The combined power of Dostoevsky and Lewis affirms Theotic Iteration's response to despair and victimhood.

The system refuses to deny the reality of violence, war, or deceit, seeing them as acute manifestations of Dissolution in the external world. When the world fails, the individual is forced into an existential battle, and the site of that battle must shift inward.

The ultimate act of resistance is not escaping the suffering, but performing an act of Iterative Change (Δ) within the suffering. The trauma is the condition, but the response is the radical choice to maintain internal integrity—the unwitnessed alignment—even when external structure is destroyed. This response affirms the ultimate reality of the Cosmic Telos (χ), the vision of transfigured creation where the pain of this life is not erased, but integrated and glorified. Both authors teach that hope is not naive optimism, but the structural, active reliance on an unbreakable Norm (Λ) that promises meaning even when all meaning seems lost.

Simone Weil: Attention, Grace, and the Pull of the Divine

Weil's concept of "attention" truly echoes the iterative approach — the disciplined, humble, and loving alignment with the eternal. Her mysticism nurtures the philosophy's insistence that knowing and creating are acts of communion, not mere cognition.
Her radical compassion and asceticism further inspire the moral and spiritual rigor of Theotic Iteration.

Summing the Synthesis

Theotic Iteration honors the radical insights and critiques of these great thinkers but answers their dilemmas by providing:
- A grounding of values in the eternal Divine Reality, avoiding nihilism.

- A faith that transcends but honors reason.
- A freedom that is dignified by given essence and purpose.
- A hope that integrates suffering into the journey of becoming like God.

It neither dismisses nor capitulates but embraces their challenges to illuminate a hopeful, practical, and intellectually sound path forward.

Aphorism:
"The void invites invention; the plenum invites praise."

Chapter X – The Summons
Life as Theotic Iteration: The Eternal Call to Creation and Communion

Introduction: The Eternal Horizon That Guides Us

If the entire human journey is one of continual iteration—
discovery, co-creation, correction—then life itself is a movement
toward God, the perfect Good, True, and Beautiful, the Ultimate
Objective Reality.

Far from being random or futile, every moment offers a choice: to
participate in the divine unfolding or to recede into dissolution.
This is the great summons—the call to become apprentices in
God's workshop, co-creators of reality, and bearers of light in a
darkened world.

The Art and Discipline of Living: Iteration as Vocation

Life is not a static possession but an ongoing art and discipline.
Each act—thought, word, deed—is an iteration: a chance to align
more closely with eternal truth or to diverge.

This vocational view rejects despair and fatalism. Iteration means
progress, flawed and nonlinear, but purposeful and directed.
It means waking daily to the responsibility and privilege of
planting seeds for eternity's harvest.

The Practical Way: Habits of Theotic Iteration

The great saints and sages translated cosmic truth into practical
habits. You cannot live this philosophy merely by thinking; you
must live it by doing.

The disciplines are many but all converge on these essentials:

- **Prayerful attention:** opening the heart and mind to hear the eternal call.
- **Intentional creation:** whether in art, work, relationships, or justice—each a sacred echo of the divine.
- **Humility and repentance:** allowing correction and learning in the face of failure.
- **Community and dialogue:** engaging others as fellow apprentices, united in the task.
- **Rest and celebration:** rejoicing in beauty as foretaste of the eternal banquet.

Freedom Fulfilled: The Joy of Alignment

Paradoxically, true freedom is found not in license but in alignment—freedom for telos, not just freedom from constraints. This freedom liberates creativity, love, and hope.

Every iteration toward God reveals deeper joy, peace, and purpose.

As Chesterton wrote with his radiant wit:
"The whole point of freedom is that you have a home to go to."

Our home is the divine order, and each act of iterated creation is a step closer to that union.

The Eternal Life of Theosis: Beyond This World's Limits

Theotic Iteration is not a philosophy of despair before death or of mere temporal accomplishment.

It points beyond this transient realm toward theosis: deification—the permanent sharing in divine life.

The process begun here, through iterative acts of creation, discovery, and sanctification, culminates in eternal communion where the soul is fully transformed in the beauty, truth, and love of God.

We are called to begin that eternal life now, in faith and works, making present the kingdom to come.

The Final Invitation: Choosing Your Seed

Each human is summoned to the ultimate decision of what seed to plant.

Will you plant seeds of life, beauty, and justice that grow forever — or seeds of bitterness, pride, and destruction that wither and die?

This philosophy demands a bold answer — a life lived bravely in creative iteration, embracing both responsibility and grace.

Final Dialogue: St. Benedict, Emerson, and Chesterton in Concert

St. Benedict:
"Let all things be done in their due measure and order, that your labor may glorify God and your soul may find peace."

Emerson:
"To trust the process and create out of love — that is to dance with the infinite and shape our own becoming."

Chesterton:
"And never forget — life is a splendid paradox. The greatest freedom is found in joyful obedience, the greatest creativity in humble imitation."

Together, they sing the final hymn of Theotic Iteration: Life is a sacred task, a divine apprenticeship, a joyous summons to endless creation.

Closing Aphorism:
"Every act can be a seed; choose what you plant, for eternity is the harvest."

Afterword: Engaging the Full Spectrum of Reality

As we close this treatise on The Philosophy of Theotic Iteration, we must turn from construction to confrontation. A philosophy that promises hope and coherence must grapple honestly with the challenges that test its very foundations. These problems are not vulnerabilities; they are the necessary friction points where the Created Reality—the Workshop—pushes back against the Eternal Blueprint—the Norm.

We address five such realities that illuminate the resilience and radical scope of our vision.

1. Animal Predation: The Non-Moral Tension of the Workshop

The reality of the natural world is defined by consuming tension: life feeds on life. This fact, often leveraged to challenge divine goodness, is understood by **Theotic Iteration** as a necessary feature of the **Temporal Workshop**.

- **The Workshop's Design:** Predation is part of the complex ecological interdependence necessary to sustain life and drive the physical cycles of preservation and renewal. It belongs to the **Created Reality**, where becoming—and thus, consuming—is inherent.

- **The Moral Boundary:** Because non-human animals lack the gift of the **Theotic Will** (free, moral agency), their suffering and death, while real, bear no **moral culpability** or **dissolution** in the human sense.

- **The Human Vocation:** We, as moral apprentices, hold the responsibility of **stewardship**—to manage this tension with ethical care, recognizing the inherent structure of the natural order without descending into needless cruelty. Predation is a non-moral iteration of renewal, not an act of gratuitous evil.

47

2. Human Conflict: The Friction of Fractured Will

The enduring record of human conflict—from personal discord to mass violence—underscores the terrifying scope of human freedom.

- **Freedom and Dissolution:** Human freedom grants **the capacity to build or to break**. Conflict is the inevitable outcome of misaligned **Theotic Wills** choosing **Dissolution** over the alignment of **Creation**.

- **Conflict as Signal:** Like suffering, conflict acts as a powerful **feedback mechanism**, signaling profound misalignment in our social and individual systems. It is the urgent, painful message that the structures of the Workshop are diverging from the Blueprint.

- **The Call to Iteration:** The resolution of conflict is the ongoing **social iteration** of dialogue, humility, repentance, and courageous co-creation. Human discord is not a denial of divine purpose, but the arduous, vital terrain on which the persistent call to unity is realized.

3. Ideological Dissolution: The Mockery of the Blueprint

The greatest challenge to our system comes from those movements—nihilism, extreme subjectivism, and transhumanism—that actively mock and seek to override the **Objective Reality** (e.g., the fixed nature of biology, logic, or truth).

- **The Purpose is Non-Being:** This mockery is the most profound form of **Dissolution**. Since the Blueprint cannot be changed, the goal is not alternative creation, but the **destruction of the self and the social order** by rejecting the very foundation of being. It is an attempt to achieve a false, self-created *pseudo-autonomy*.

- **Origin in Failed Iteration:** This perverse will stems from the tragic convergence of **epistemological failure** (the mind rejecting the feedback of Reason and Sense) and **moral failure** (the will choosing pride and hatred over humility and love).

- **The Inescapable Constraint:** Their fanatical hatred of the Norm ironically validates the Norm's power. Their eventual failure is the loudest possible **Signal**—a testament to the fact that the **Core Algorithm** cannot be broken, only tragically ignored.

4. The Limits of Human Knowledge and Fallibility

If reality is intelligible, why are human beings so consistently mistaken, falling victim to historical and personal error?

- **Knowledge is an Iteration:** Our certainty lies in the **Theotic Axiom** (reality is intelligible), not in our current grasp of it. Knowledge is a humble, communal, and **multi-nodal process**—a progressive approximation always seeking, never fully exhausted.

- **Humility Before Mystery:** Our human vocation is defined by navigating the paradox between finite reason and infinite truth. Fallibility is the inherent friction of the Apprentice, driving us toward disciplined effort and trust in **the ultimate, unconditioned source of being**.

- **Certainty in Participation:** True certainty is not a logical conquest but an ontological reward; it grows only as our participation deepens. The goal is to align with the truth, not merely possess it.

5. The Problem of Relativism and Cultural Conflict

How can a claim of **Objective Reality** accommodate the immense diversity of human cultures without leading to authoritarian imposition?

- **Universal Norm, Diverse Expression:** The **Objective Reality** is universal and immutable, but the human **participation and cultural expression** of that truth is historically and geographically variant. The Blueprint is one; the architecture of the Workshop is diverse.

- **The Call for Dialogue:** Genuine dialogue requires intellectual humility: recognizing the validity of partial, local perspectives without falling into the relativistic lie that the Norm itself is pliable.

- **Invitation to Goodness: Theotic Iteration** does not call for imperial imposition. It calls for **convincing witness**—demonstrating the beauty, peace, and productivity that naturally arise when a culture chooses **Creation** over **Dissolution**. The system's spread relies on its power to attract, not its power to compel.

Closing Reflection

These challenges—hard truths of nature, social fractures, ideological hostility, human limits, and cultural plurality—do not weaken The Philosophy of Theotic Iteration. They illuminate its strength. It is a philosophy that embraces the tension of the Workshop, grounding its hope in the fidelity of the Eternal Blueprint.

It does not promise instant perfection, but a lifelong, courageous journey of iterative partnership—a promise that every creative act, great or small, matters eternally.

Aphorism:
"In the theater of creation, every trial and triumph is but another act in the eternal dance of Becoming and Being."

Afterword II: The Philosophy Against Dissolution

A philosophy grounded in the Theotic Axiom and the certainty of Objective Reality (Ω) cannot afford the luxury of intellectual neutrality. If our core premise is that existence is defined by the Moral Axis of Creation versus Dissolution, then we must explicitly name and confront those systems and thinkers whose work actively serves the project of collapse.

This philosophy is not syncretic. It is not ecumenical. It is an absolute claim that sets itself in direct opposition to any worldview—secular or religious—that denies the Eternal Blueprint or replaces the divine Telos of Theosis (χ) with a subjective, worldly alternative.

1. The Foundations of Ontological Failure

The modern descent into Dissolution began not with the corruption of ethics, but with the corruption of first principles—a total failure to recognize the nature and limits of the Objective Reality.

The Cartesian Collapse was the initial philosophical wound, self-inflicted by thinkers like René Descartes, whose "I think, therefore I am" collapsed the foundation of being from the Personal Absolute (Ω) into the isolated subject. This placed pseudo-autonomy at the center of existence, suggesting individual consciousness is the ground of truth, rather than an instrument for discerning the truth already provided by the Logos (Λ). The later failure, epitomized by the Linguistic Trap of thinkers like Wittgenstein, confused the map for the territory.

By asserting that reality is merely a function of language games or social construction, they decoupled Created Reality from the

51

Objective Norm (Λ), making truth perpetually contingent. Our philosophy holds that the Logos precedes the word: language is a tool for apprehending truth, not the mechanism for generating it.

2. The Architects of Dissolution: A Critique of the Subjective Will

The failure of first principles empowered a generation of theorists who dedicated themselves to the comprehensive breakdown of structure—intellectual, moral, and social—in the name of "liberation."

The most insidious failure was anthropological, rejecting the arduous work of the Apprentice of God for the Cult of the Primitive. Rousseau's Error asserted that man is naturally good (The Noble Savage) and is corrupted only by society. This Primitive Lie rejects the reality of the inherent Dissolution in the human heart and attempts to replace the hard work of Iteration (Δ) with a return to a non-existent state of pure instinct. This intellectual fantasy was popularized by figures like Margaret Mead, validating the ache for the beastial—the primal urge to shed the complex, disciplined structure of civilization and return to unreflective appetite.

Building on the Primitive Lie, the Agents of Chaos—Foucault, Derrida, the Frankfurt School, Freud, Kinsey, and Laing—became the architects of total deconstruction. Systems of Critical Theory are dedicated to Diabolical Inversion, defining Creation (order, family, tradition) as oppression and seeking only to dismantle. Post-Structuralism (Foucault, Derrida) denied the existence of a stable Logos, condemning the Theotic Will to subjective, meaningless wandering. The Pathologists of the Soul (Freud, Kinsey, Laing) radically reduced the human person, prioritizing pathology and base instinct over spiritual vocation. They define man downward, denying his capacity for the sublime work of Creation.

The entire project of this intellectual current is structurally invalidated by Theotic Iteration. A man who understands the fixed laws of physics and engineering well enough to build his own house and purify his own water—an act of genuine, rigorous Creation—has a profound, earned grasp of Objective Reality (Ω) that is worth more than every line of abstract, disintegrative theory ever written by the Frankfurt School.

3. Symptoms and the Theotic Response to Despair

When a culture embraces the Primitive Lie and rejects the Eternal Blueprint, the Created Reality—the Workshop—begins to visibly decay. This decay is not just abstract; it manifests as the real-world injustices of war, violence, deceit, and personal despair.

The system addresses this despair by clarifying the relationship between the External World (governed by Dissolution) and the Internal Will (governed by Iteration).

The Reorientation of the Moral Axis

When one is victimized, the external world has failed the Moral Axis (Λ). The core failure of the modern self is to tie its worth to the stability of the external world. The Theotic Insight is that Iteration (Δ) is measured solely by the unwitnessed integrity of the agent's response, not by the event's outcome. Despair is the surrender to Dissolution—the belief that the self must scatter because the world has scattered. The system requires an act of Theotic Will to maintain internal structure even when the external structure is obliterated. The moral measure is not Did I prevent the harm? but Did I choose the most difficult alignment with the Norm (Λ) in the face of the harm?

The Fallow Cycle as Radical Preservation

In moments of deep trauma, the Effort Cycle is impossible and inappropriate. The system demands that the agent enter an extended, necessary Fallow Cycle, but views this withdrawal not as collapse, but as radical, disciplined self-preservation. The Refusal of False Comfort means the Fallow Cycle is not escapism. It is the practice of preserving the Theotic Will by demanding deliberate rest and stillness—the Linger-Spot is a defense against the world's chaos. The Fallow Book becomes the absolute primary form of Iteration (Δ) during trauma, rebuilding internal intelligibility by recording the quiet, intentional acts of self-structure that refuse to surrender to the chaos.

The Transcendent Value of Form (The χ Telos)

For Theotic Iteration, suffering is understood in the context of the ultimate Cosmic Telos (χ)—the promise of the Transfiguration of Creation. If the final destiny is the Glorification of Form, then every action of integrity performed within this life holds permanent value. The system asserts that the victim's Moral

Alignment during suffering is a far more profound act of co-creation than the aggressor's act of destruction. The victim's choice to maintain internal Λ-alignment is an act of universal, enduring Δ.

The philosophy does not promise a quick emotional healing, but it provides a structural reason to continue the work. It shifts the focus from the loss of external assets (peace, safety, property) to the preservation of the internal, unwitnessed integrity — the one asset that can never be stolen.

Closing Summons to Rigor

The Signal of suffering and dissolution is painful, but it is grace. It is the inescapable proof that the Blueprint (Λ) is still intact.

Our calling is not to mourn the chaos but to engage in the courageous, disciplined work of Creation (Δ), restoring Integrity, Proportion, and Radiance to the places that chaos has claimed. The work begins with the self and moves outward, one rigorous Iteration at a time.

Final Aphorism:
"The lie can be written in a thousand books, but the truth is built by the man who can trust the physics of his own two hands."

Author's Note: The Philosophy's Place and Purpose

A philosophy grounded in the Theotic Axiom and the certainty of an Objective Reality (Ω) cannot afford the luxury of intellectual neutrality. If our core premise is that existence is **defined by the Moral Axis of Creation versus Dissolution**, then the work itself must be an explicit intervention in the current philosophical landscape.

1. The Context: A Necessary Anti-Nihilistic Treaty

This work is intended as **an anti-nihilistic treaty**—a complete system offered in response to the relativistic and subjective currents that have dominated Western thought since the nineteenth century. Its core purpose is to provide a firm foundation for meaning and moral structure without demanding intellectual regression.

The Philosophy of Theotic Iteration is not syncretic. It is an absolute claim that sets itself in direct opposition to any worldview—secular or religious—that denies the Eternal Blueprint (Λ) or replaces the divine *Telos* of *Theosis* (χ) with a subjective, worldly alternative. Its utility stems from its powerful ability to affirm the objectivity of Truth, Goodness, and Beauty, offering a hopeful and robust metaphysics for the modern crisis of fragmentation and purposelessness.

2. Originality Through Synthesis: The New Architecture

While this philosophy is rigorously original, intellectual honesty demands the acknowledgment that no comprehensive system is built *ex nihilo*. The concepts of Theosis, Actus Purus, and the nature of moral evil are foundational bricks inherited from deep traditions. The originality of this system lies not in inventing those bricks, but in the architecture—the novel way they are combined to form a coherent, dynamic structure.

The system achieves near-maximal originality by performing three key acts of synthesis

1. **The Activation of Theosis (Δ):** It transforms the theological concept of θ∈οσιο (deification) from a passive spiritual goal into an active, iterative, and vocational methodology. **Theotic Iteration** (Δ) is the core mechanism that binds metaphysics, ethics, and epistemology together.

2. **The Theistic Answer to Modernity:** It directly engages the challenge of the "Will to Power" by re-framing it as the **Theotic Will**—an intrinsic drive toward mastery that finds its fulfillment only in disciplined co-creation with the eternal Norm (Λ). This provides a grounded, non-reactionary, positive anthropology.

3. **Dynamic Metaphysics:** It takes the static distinctions of Thomism (Ω) and Palamism (Essence/Energies) and makes them dynamic (Objective Reality/Created Reality), creating an ontological framework that is fully compatible with modern iterative processes (design, science, craft).

    The result is a system so distinct in its language, structure, and mechanism that it has never been articulated before, earning its place as a new voice in philosophical discourse.

3. The Achievement: A Unified Life Vocation

The greatest achievement of this philosophy is its capacity to offer a unified life vocation that resists the modern urge toward compartmentalization.

It doesn't ask the reader to live as a scientist on weekdays and a mystic on weekends; it shows how science, art, ethics, and spirituality are all integrated acts of **co-creation** (Δ) within the **Temporal Workshop**.

*   **Objective Ethics:** By grounding morality in ontological affirmation (**The Moral Axis**), it ensures that values are objective and measurable, directly opposing contemporary relativism.

- **Positive Theodicy:** The framing of **Suffering as Signal** provides a robust and deeply useful answer to the problem of evil. It transforms pain from a random curse into a corrective message demanding an iterative response (healing, repentance, resistance), giving profound structural meaning to personal despair.

- **Actionable Metaphysics:** The system provides a clear mandate for life: institutions and personal efforts should be judged by how well they enable and protect the iterative vocation of the soul.

The goal is not merely to describe this synthesis, but to provide the tools for its immediate reversal of personal and social decay. The philosophy is intellectually rigorous, theologically profound, and practically empowering.

Final Aphorism:
"The lie can be written in a thousand books, but the truth is built by the man who can trust the physics of his own two hands."

www.ingramcontent.com/pod-product-compliance
Lightning Source LLC
Chambersburg PA
CBHW020810130626
46554CB00006B/2374